# GET OUT OF YOUR HEAD!

Empowering Strategies for Conquering Low self-esteem, Anxieties, Phobias, Self-Sabotage, Depression and Enhancing Overall Mental Well-Being

By

Gretel C. McGuffin

Copyright @2023

# TABLE OF CONTENT


**CHAPTER ONE** ...............................................5

Phobias and Low Self-Esteem ...................5

Fear and Anxiety....................................12

The Effects of Fear and Anxiety ..............16

**CHAPTER TWO** ..............................................19

Exploring Different Types of Anxiety and Phobias.................................................19

Social Anxiety Disorder (SAD) .................28

Methods Via Which Children Acquire Social Anxiety.......................................30

**CHAPTER THREE** ....................................33

Childhood Behavioral Inhibition .............33

Triggers of Social Anxiety .......................38

Approaches for Handling Social Anxiety .42

Different Forms of Depression ..................50

**CHAPTER FOUR**............................................53

**Treatment Options for Anxiety** ...............53

**Post-Traumatic Stress Disorder (PTSD)**..64

**CHAPTER FIVE** ...........................................67

**Low Self-esteem or Lacking Confidence in Oneself** ...................................................67

**Strategies for Boosting Self-Confidence**...68

**Addressing Low Self-Esteem Issues** .........75

**CHAPTER SIX** ............................................87

**Diet, Exercise, Physical Activities and Mental Well-being**....................................87

**Impact of Nutritional Regimen on Mental Health**..................................................91

**END**........................................................97

Do you hold a consistently low opinion of yourself? Or do you hold the persistent belief that you are deserving of neither praise nor commendation, but rather an underachiever? If this is the case, you may be experiencing diminished self-esteem.

A phobia refers to the irrational arousal of worry in response to a particular circumstance or object, it impedes one's daily functioning, and the resulting dread may be so intense that one will do anything to avoid the object of the phobia. Debilitating phobias fall under the category of anxiety disorders. Debilitating and detrimental phobias can prevent you from sharing your favorite activities with your loved ones. Nevertheless, this need not be the case. Low self-esteem can color our entire lives, whether it's considering ourselves doomed to fail at something and failing to put forth our best effort, believing that no one could truly love us and consequently alienating ourselves from our partners, or accepting poor treatment simply because a small portion of us believes we deserve it.

Additionally, as a viscous cycle ensues, the consequences of these behaviors may validate our deepest self-doubts. There is hope and help for everyone with anxiety, phobias and self-esteem issues.

This comprehensive guide explores the underlying factors that contribute to low self-esteem, phobias, depression and anxiety, specifically focusing on these difficulties from early childhood through adolescence and into adulthood.

# CHAPTER ONE

## Phobias and Low Self-Esteem

During my adolescence, I grappled with a self-esteem crisis stemming from the belief that I lacked beauty; I constantly felt inadequate, unattractive, and underbuilt. It took my mother an extended period of time to assist me in regaining my confidence, and it was my first boyfriend at the age of nineteen who validated what my mother had been attempting to convey for years. At this time, I am married to my exceptional man who elevates my self-esteem and beauty at each opportunity.

A phobia is a strong and illogical fear of a certain thing or circumstance. A phobia is categorized as an anxiety condition, as the primary symptom experienced by the sufferer is anxiety. Phobias are believed to be acquired emotional reactions. Phobias are commonly believed to arise when the dread experienced in an initial dangerous scenario is transferred to other similar situations, frequently with the original fear being suppressed or forgotten. Hydrophobia, an irrational dread of water, can stem from a repressed childhood memory of nearly drowning. The sufferer thus endeavors to evade that circumstance in subsequent instances, a reaction that, although alleviating worry in the immediate term, strengthens the individual's connection between the condition and the onset of anxiety.

Behaviour therapy frequently achieves success in overcoming phobias. In this form of therapy, the individual with a phobia is systematically and gradually exposed to the object or circumstance that causes anxiety.

This exposure is done in a controlled manner until the person no longer experiences anxiety. Through this process, the individual comes to recognize that their anxious expectations of the situation are not fulfilled. By breaking the strong connections between the dreaded circumstance, the person's sensation of anxiety, and their subsequent avoidance of that situation, a less harmful set of reactions is established. Psychotherapy can be beneficial for addressing phobias. Psychiatrists categorize phobias as a specific sort of anxiety disorder. However, other terms have been created to describe the specific nature of the fear by combining "phobia" with the Greek word for the dreaded item. Some notable examples of phobias are acrophobia (fear of high places), claustrophobia (fear of closed places), nyctophobia (fear of the dark), ochlophobia (fear of crowds), xenophobia (fear of strangers), and zoophobia (fear of animals). Agoraphobia, an intense fear of open or public spaces, is a debilitating condition that can severely restrict individuals from venturing outside their homes. School fear may affect pupils who have an excessive attachment to a parent.

**Acrophobia** is a strong and irrational fear of heights. Individuals afflicted with acrophobia experience severe fear and anxiety when at a significant height above the earth, such as in elevated parking garages or on bridges, or when contemplating being at a significant height above the ground. Individuals with acrophobia may suffer from panic attacks when exposed to triggering conditions, leading them to intentionally avoid these scenarios. Acrophobia can also be defined as a cognitive condition characterized by an exaggerated perception of threat in a given setting.

The etiology of acrophobia remains uncertain. The condition may be influenced by a hereditary predisposition. For instance, the presence of acrophobia or an anxiety disorder in one family member may result in others within the family experiencing comparable fear and anxiety, indicating a potential hereditary component. Navigation theory explores an additional potential explanation of acrophobia, proposing that individuals may perceive objects as being at a greater height than they truly are, leading to a fear of falling and subsequent panic. This misjudgment of height is believed to stem from evolutionary adaptation. Engaging in excessive contemplation of the possible discomfort that may arise after a fall can lead to the emergence of the condition. Acrophobia can also be associated with a distressing event related to elevated positions. For instance, an individual who has a sudden episode of intense fear when in a tall location may subsequently acquire acrophobia, even if the fear of heights and the panic attack were previously unrelated. The symptoms of acrophobia typically manifest as both physical and psychological in character. Physical manifestations may encompass perspiration, quivering or trembling, vertigo, faintness, constriction or discomfort in the thoracic region, heightened cardiac rhythm, or a sensation of nausea. Psychological symptoms encompass sensations of panic, intense anxiety, and a want to escape the current circumstances. Individuals who are affected may have an intense feeling of fear when faced with the possibility of a negative result while being at a significant height, such as falling or being unable to descend. The cognitive processes and early manifestations of acrophobia bear resemblance to those observed in panic disorder. Individuals diagnosed with panic disorder exhibit a proclivity to see ordinary body experiences as menacing. Similarly, an individual with acrophobia perceives the physical feelings felt at elevated locations encountered in daily life as potentially hazardous. Hence, the perception of elevated positions is associated with detrimental cognitive processes and potential physical injury. A feedback loop is therefore formed, where the trigger of being elevated induces worry, leading to heightened bodily symptoms and negative cognitive patterns, which in turn can further intensify anxiety.

# Fear and Anxiety

Anxiety is an emotional state characterized by a sense of unease, worry, or fear, typically without any specific or rational cause. Anxiety is differentiated from fear due to the fact that fear is triggered by a tangible and immediate threat, such as a situation that poses a risk to a person's physical well-being. Anxiety, on the other hand, occurs in reaction to seemingly harmless situations or is the result of personal, internal emotional problems whose origins may not be obvious to the individual. Occasional anxiety is an inherent part of everyday living and is generally considered to be within the normal range. However, anxiety that is continuous, acute, chronic, or recurring and is not warranted by real-life circumstances is typically considered indicative of an emotional condition.

Generalized anxiety, also known as free-floating anxiety, refers to a state of diffuse or persistent unease that is not specifically linked to any single cause or mental issue. There are numerous factors and psychological reasons behind anxiety. Anxiety can stem from situations that challenge an individual's sense of self-worth, such as feeling inadequate in sexual or job-related matters. Anxiety is seen by behavioral psychologists as a response that is learned through real-life experiences. This anxiety becomes connected to the specific circumstances surrounding the event, causing those circumstances to independently trigger anxiety in the person. Personality and social psychologists have observed that when individuals perceive stimuli as threatening or dangerous, it can lead to the development or persistence of anxiety.

A potential consequence of ineffective anxiety management is the development of an anxiety disorder, which manifests as a persistent or recurring state of anxiety or general fear that is not limited to specific situations or objects. The tension often manifests as difficulty sleeping, sudden bursts of irritability, restlessness, rapid heartbeats, and concerns about one's mental or physical well-being.

Tiredness is commonly felt when too much energy is spent on dealing with overwhelming anxiety. Sometimes, the anxiety can manifest in a more intense way, leading to physical symptoms like nausea, diarrhea, frequent urination, feelings of suffocation, dilated pupils, sweating, or rapid breathing.

Similar indications can be observed in various physiological disorders and in typical situations of stress or fear. However, when these indications arise without any underlying organic defect or pathology, and in situations that most individuals handle effortlessly, they may be deemed neurotic.

# The Effects of Fear and Anxiety

Anxiety and depression are common experiences that many people face at different times in their lives. During certain situations, anxiety can be a natural response that helps you approach a challenging or stressful situation with added caution and care. It's completely normal to experience feelings of loneliness, sadness, or disinterest when confronted with challenging, life-altering situations.

However, when mental health conditions such as anxiety start to disrupt daily life and persistent feelings of overwhelming sadness or emptiness arise, it becomes more than just a result of life circumstances - it becomes a mental health disorder.

Fear, a common human emotion, arises when we perceive a potential threat. Our bodies have a natural instinct to react when faced with danger, triggering a fight or flight response. Therefore, it plays a crucial role in ensuring our safety.

Nevertheless, individuals who find themselves living in a state of perpetual fear, whether due to tangible dangers in their surroundings or perceived threats, may encounter adverse consequences across various aspects of their existence, potentially leading to a state of incapacitation. Being aware of potential threats helps us to respond effectively. When our body detects a possible threat, it responds by releasing hormones that can slow down or even temporarily halt certain bodily functions that are not essential for immediate survival, such as our digestive system.

Enhance functions that can aid in our survival, like eyesight. As our heart rate rises, blood rushes to our muscles, allowing us to increase our speed. Our body also enhances the flow of hormones to a specific area of the brain called the amygdala, which aids in our ability to concentrate on the imminent threat and retain it in our memory.

# CHAPTER TWO

## Exploring Different Types of Anxiety and Phobias

Anxiety disorders are a common mental health condition characterized by excessive worry and fear. They can significantly impact a person's daily life and overall well-being. One specific type of anxiety disorder is generalized anxiety disorder (GAD). GAD typically entails a continuous sense of anxiety or apprehension that can disrupt one's daily routine. There is a distinction between occasional worries and anxiety caused by stressful life events. Individuals with Generalized Anxiety Disorder often endure persistent anxiety that can last for extended periods of time, sometimes spanning months or even years.

Symptoms of Generalized Anxiety Disorder (GAD) may include:

- Sense of restlessness, agitation, or unease
- Feeling tired easily Struggling to stay focused
- Feeling a bit cranky
- Experiencing headaches, muscle aches, stomachaches, or unexplained pains
- Struggling to manage overwhelming feelings of concern
- Experiencing sleep issues, like struggling to fall or stay asleep

**Panic Disorder**

Individuals who experience panic disorder often face frequent and unpredictable episodes of panic attacks. Panic attacks can strike unexpectedly, causing overwhelming fear and a feeling of losing control, even in the absence of any apparent danger or trigger. Panic disorder is not a guaranteed outcome for everyone who goes through a panic attack.

During a panic attack, individuals may go through the following symptoms:

- Heart palpitations
- Perspiring
- Shaking or prickling
- Experiencing chest pain
- Sense of impending disaster
- Sensations of losing control

Individuals with panic disorder frequently experience concerns about the timing of their next panic attack and make conscious efforts to avoid places, situations, or behaviors that they associate with these episodes. It is possible for panic attacks to happen frequently, happening multiple times a day, or they can occur infrequently, only happening a few times a year.

## Social Anxiety Disorder

Social anxiety disorder is a psychological condition characterized by an intense fear and avoidance of social situations. Social anxiety disorder is a profound and enduring fear of being observed and evaluated by others. Individuals suffering with social anxiety disorder experience an overwhelming and uncontrollable level of apprehension towards social situations. For certain individuals, this phobia can hinder their ability to engage in employment, education, or routine activities.

Individuals afflicted with social anxiety disorder may encounter the following symptoms:

- Facial redness, perspiration, or bodily shaking
- Tachycardia
- Abdominal pain
- Adopting a stiff bodily stance or speaking with an excessively gentle voice
- Challenges in establishing eye contact or feeling comfortable in the presence of unfamiliar individuals.
- Experiencing self-consciousness or apprehension around potential negative judgments from others.

**Disorders Associated to Phobias**

While it is understandable to have anxiety in certain situations, individuals with phobias exhibit a dread that is disproportionate to the actual level of risk posed by the specific situation or object.

**Individuals afflicted with a phobia:**

May have a heightened and disproportionate concern or anxiety around the possibility of coming into contact with the object or circumstance that is dreaded. Employ proactive measures to evade the object or circumstance that instills fear.

Specific phobias, often known as simple phobias: Individuals with a specific phobia experience a profound and overwhelming fear or anxiety towards particular things or circumstances, as indicated by the name.

Specific phobias encompass various fears, such as:

- Aerial Elevations
- Particular creatures, such as arachnids, canines, or serpents
- Administering injections
- Blood

Social anxiety disorder, formerly known as social phobia, is characterized by individuals experiencing a pervasive and strong dread or anxiety in social or performance-related situations. Individuals with anxiety are concerned that their actions or behaviors related to their anxiety may be subject to negative evaluation by others, resulting in feelings of embarrassment. Individuals with social anxiety frequently abstain from social gatherings due to this concern. Social anxiety disorder can present itself in several contexts, including professional settings and educational institutions.

Separation anxiety disorder: Separation anxiety is commonly perceived as a phenomenon exclusive to children. Nevertheless, separation anxiety disorder can also be identified in adults. others afflicted with separation anxiety disorder experience intense apprehension when they are physically separated from others with whom they share a close emotional bond. They frequently experience anxiety around potential harm befalling their loved ones during periods of separation. This dread causes individuals to actively avoid solitude or separation from their loved ones. They may experience distressing dreams or physical discomfort in anticipation of separation.

Selective mutism is a relatively uncommon condition that is linked to anxiety. Selective mutism is a condition in which individuals are unable to speak in some social contexts, even though they possess typical language abilities. Selective mutism typically manifests prior to the age of 5 and is frequently linked to profound timidity, apprehension of social humiliation, obsessive tendencies, seclusion, dependency, and outbursts of anger. Individuals diagnosed with selective mutism frequently receive concurrent diagnoses of other anxiety disorders.

# Social Anxiety Disorder (SAD)

If you have received a diagnosis of social anxiety disorder (SAD), you might be curious about the factors that contributed to the development of this condition. The condition is most likely caused by a complex interaction of various factors, rather than a single cause.

## Genetic

If you have been diagnosed with Seasonal Affective Disorder (SAD), it is likely that you possess certain genetic traits that increase your susceptibility to acquiring this condition. If you have a close family member with Social Anxiety Disorder (SAD), your chances of developing the disorder may increase by two to six times. Heritability refers to the extent to which genetic differences across people contribute to the variance observed in a phenotype, such as traits, characteristics, or physical features.

The residual variation is commonly ascribed to environmental influences. Studies on heritability generally assess the relative influence of genetic and environmental variables on a specific trait or characteristic.

## Ecological

The etiology of social anxiety disorder (SAD) encompasses psychosocial elements present in one's developmental environment. If an individual has a parent who suffers from social anxiety disorder (SAD), they are at an increased likelihood of developing the same disorder. This phenomenon may be attributed to a combination of hereditary and environmental factors.

## Methods Via Which Children Acquire Social Anxiety

Did you fail to remember your lines during the theatrical performance in class? Were you subjected to ridicule or incessant harassment by other children? Although not essential, experiencing an early traumatic event can potentially influence the later development of social anxiety, even after several years.

Observational learning: Have you witnessed someone else undergoing a terrible social scenario if you have not personally experienced it? For individuals who are already susceptible to the illness, this may have an equivalent effect to experiencing the incident directly.

# Data Transmission

Anxious parents, who experience fear and social anxiety, unintentionally communicate both verbally and non-verbally to their children about the potential risks associated with social interactions. If your mother exhibits a high level of concern with the opinions of others, it is likely that you have also acquired some degree of this anxiety. The probability of developing SAD might also be influenced by your background.

Your likelihood of developing the disease increases if:

> During your childhood, you lacked sufficient exposure to social situations and were restricted from developing adequate social skills.

> Either one or both of your parents exhibited traits of rejection, control, criticism, or overprotection.

➢ Children who fail to establish a secure attachment with their primary caregiver are more vulnerable since they lack the ability to self-regulate and find solace in challenging circumstances.

# CHAPTER THREE

## Childhood Behavioral Inhibition

Do you know a toddler or young child who always becomes severely distressed when confronted with a new environment or strange person? When confronted with such circumstances, does the youngster exhibit crying, withdrawal, or seek solace from a parent? The term used to describe this kind of conduct in toddlers and young children is behavioral inhibition. Toddlers that exhibit behavioral restraint have an increased susceptibility to developing Social Anxiety Disorder (SAD) in the future. Given its early manifestation, this temperament is presumably an innate trait influenced by biological causes.

When parents exhibit excessive control, readily criticize, display reluctance in showing affection, or excessively prioritize the views of others, a child's self-image and perception of the world might be influenced by the verbal expressions and behaviors associated with these traits.

Children and adolescents raised in this atmosphere may have heightened fearfulness and diminished trust in others. Additionally, their self-esteem and self-confidence may be adversely affected. Parents often fail to recognize the detrimental effects of their behavior in these situations. However, their over emphasis on the bad aspects can unintentionally create difficulties for their children in the future. The diagnosis of social anxiety disorder typically occurs in adults, although symptoms often appear during late childhood or early adolescence.

This suggests that parental factors may play a significant role in the creation of the illness.

Social Anxiety Disorder and the Brain Neuroimaging studies have demonstrated that individuals with social anxiety disorder exhibit heightened neural activity in the amygdala, a specific region of the brain. The amygdala is accountable for the physiological alterations linked to the "flight-or-fight" reaction, which activates the body to react to perceived dangers, whether they are genuine or imagined.

The activation of the amygdala initiates a cascade of symptoms associated with severe anxiety, such as increased heart rate, sweaty palms, heightened respiration, muscle tension, elevated blood sugar levels, and cognitive impairment that impairs normal thinking and reasoning abilities in individuals experiencing anxiety.

During episodes of heightened anxiety, individuals' cognitive attention is directed towards the prefrontal cortex, a specific region of the brain. The prefrontal cortex is responsible for regulating emotional reactions by evaluating them logically and calmly. If there is no actual danger, it is expected to transmit messages to the amygdala to alleviate its anxious response. However, individuals with social anxiety experience a phenomenon where the prefrontal cortex intensifies the activity of the amygdala instead of reducing it. Individuals suffering from social anxiety possess a deeply ingrained dread of how others may respond, causing their brains to perceive social interactions as genuine dangers. Despite attempts at logical reasoning, these worries cannot be entirely alleviated.

Thankfully, the human brain has the ability to be reprogrammed to create new neural pathways and establish connections regardless of one's age. Through the utilization of cognitive-behavioral therapy, which is the favored therapeutic approach for social anxiety, individuals diagnosed with social anxiety disorder can effectively recondition their cognitive processes to respond in a more logical and thoughtful manner when faced with social situations that do not pose any genuine threat.

## Triggers of Social Anxiety

Not all social situations trigger symptoms of social anxiety for individuals who are affected by it. When engaging with individuals they have established relationships with and have a high level of confidence in—such as partners, parents, siblings, children, grandparents, close friends, long-time employers, favorite teachers, and so on—they may exhibit no indications of social anxiety at all. Furthermore, when called upon to address topics within their area of expertise or where they have a proven track record, they might possess a certain level of self-assurance.

However, numerous other circumstances can elicit significant distress and anxiety, despite appearing non-threatening to the majority of individuals. There are certain factors that can often cause distress for individuals with social anxiety:

- ➢ Encountering unfamiliar individuals

- ➢ Relationships

- ➢ Engaging with individuals in positions of power

- ➢ Interactions with individuals who are more outgoing

- ➢ Parties can be quite challenging, particularly for individuals who experience social anxiety

- ➢ Large family gatherings where not everyone is acquainted

- ➢ Surprising encounters with individuals seeking to engage in conversations in public settings, such as while waiting in line at the bank or grocery store

➤ Experiencing playful banter or jesting (individuals with social anxiety disorder may interpret teasing as personal)

➤ Under close observation while attempting a novel or unfamiliar task

➤ Being given the opportunity to address a class or a group of colleagues

➤ Engaging in telephone conversations, particularly with individuals one is not familiar with

➤ Therapy sessions or support groups for social anxiety can present challenges for individuals who struggle with opening up and expressing their emotions in these environments.

➢ Many individuals who experience social anxiety disorder tend to have specific situations that elicit intense feelings of anxiety. They often go to great lengths to avoid these situations whenever possible. Other social situations can sometimes lead to feelings of discomfort and hinder daily life.

## Approaches for Handling Social Anxiety

**Dealing with social situations:** It is important to recognize areas where one's social skills could benefit from improvement when dealing with social anxiety disorder. By prioritizing the enhancement of those aspects, it could potentially assist in managing the thoughts and emotions associated with social anxiety disorder.

**Sharing Your Social Anxiety with Others:** It's probable that those closest to you are already aware of your social anxiety. If you wish to communicate with someone in a thoughtful manner, consider sending them a message expressing your desire to share something important. Then, suggest meeting at a peaceful location to engage in a conversation. If you find yourself hesitant to articulate your circumstances, consider jotting down a concise overview of your emotions. It is advisable to communicate your symptoms in order to help the other person understand your situation.

**Relaxing Breathing Techniques:** Experiencing social anxiety often leads to intense emotional responses in social settings. One method to alleviate these anxious reactions is for your body to be in a state of relaxation. When your body is at ease, your breathing becomes calm and effortless, allowing your mind to be clear of any negativity. This creates a more pleasant atmosphere for social interactions. In anxiety-provoking situations, it's possible that your breathing rate increases, which can exacerbate other symptoms of anxiety.

**Confronting Your Anxieties:** Steering clear of situations that cause apprehension may provide temporary relief from emotional responses, yet ultimately, it significantly constrains one's life. Furthermore, the range of situations that cause concern expands as your apprehension becomes more widespread. Alternatively, by gradually immersing yourself in social situations and practicing relaxation techniques, you can effectively diminish the anxiety and emotional responses that are linked to those specific situations.

**Depression:** In psychology, depression is characterized by a mood or emotional state that involves feelings of low self-worth or guilt, as well as a diminished capacity to experience joy in life. When someone is feeling down, they may go through a range of symptoms such as sadness, low self-esteem, and a lack of enjoyment in everyday activities. They may also experience a decrease in energy, slower thinking or movement, changes in appetite, and difficulty sleeping. Depression is distinct from ordinary grief or mourning, as it is a suitable emotional reaction to the absence of cherished individuals or possessions.

The classification of depression into different types is based on the distinctions in duration, circumstances of onset, and other specific characteristics. There are various types of depression, such as bipolar disorder, major depressive disorder (clinical depression), persistent depressive disorder, and seasonal affective disorder.

There are various factors that can contribute to depression. Challenging life circumstances have the potential to heighten an individual's susceptibility to depression or initiate a depressive episode. It is worth noting that negative thoughts about oneself and the world play a significant role in generating and sustaining depressive symptoms. Nevertheless, it is evident that both psychosocial and biochemical mechanisms play significant roles in the development of this condition. Specifically, the defective regulation of the release of certain neurotransmitters in the brain, such as norepinephrine and serotonin, seems to be a key biochemical factor. It is believed that a decrease in the levels or functioning of these chemicals in the brain can contribute to the development of a depressed mood in certain individuals.

# The Causes of Depression

There are multiple potential factors that contribute to depression. They can vary from biological to circumstantial.

- Neurotransmitters and their effects on the brain. It is possible that certain areas of the brain responsible for regulating mood, thoughts, sleep, appetite, and behavior may experience a chemical imbalance in individuals with depression.

- Levels of hormones. Fluctuations in female hormones estrogen and progesterone throughout various stages such as the menstrual cycle, postpartum period, perimenopause, or menopause can potentially increase the likelihood of experiencing depression.

- Ancestral lineage. If there is a history of depression or another mood disorder in your family, it may increase your susceptibility to developing depression.

- Experiences from early childhood that have had a lasting impact. Certain occurrences can influence how your body responds to fear and stressful circumstances.

- Structure of the brain. It is worth noting that a less active frontal lobe of the brain may increase the susceptibility to depression. However, it remains uncertain whether this occurs prior to or following the emergence of depressive symptoms.

- Health issues. There are certain factors that may increase your vulnerability, such as chronic illness, insomnia, chronic pain, Parkinson's disease, stroke, heart attack, and cancer.

- Substance use. Your risk can be influenced by a history of substance or alcohol misuse.

- Discomfort. Individuals experiencing prolonged emotional or chronic physical pain are at a higher risk of developing depression.

# Different Forms of Depression

The main types of depression include bipolar disorder, major depressive disorder, and persistent depressive disorder. Individuals who go through fluctuating periods of depression and mania or hypomania are diagnosed with bipolar disorder. Major depressive disorder is marked by significant symptoms that greatly impact a person's daily life, often affecting their appetite, sleep, work, and overall enjoyment of life. Episodes of major depression can manifest at any age and may occur intermittently throughout an individual's life.

Persistent depressive disorder is characterized by symptoms that persist for two or more years, occasionally accompanied by episodes of major depression.

There are various types of depression that can arise in different situations, such as postpartum depression, psychotic depression, and seasonal affective disorder. Postpartum depression can occur in women after giving birth. Common signs may involve feelings of unease, diminished motivation to attend to the infant's needs, and experiencing emotions of melancholy, despair, or self-doubt.

Postpartum depression is a more intense and enduring condition compared to the "baby blues," which is a common experience among women after giving birth and often includes mood swings, feelings of sadness, and episodes of crying.

Psychotic depression occurs in the presence of psychosis, which can manifest as delusions, hallucinations, or paranoia. Seasonal affective disorder is characterized by the onset of depressive symptoms in autumn and winter, which can be relieved by increased exposure to natural light in spring and summer.

# CHAPTER FOUR

## Treatment Options for Anxiety

Anxiety disorders are commonly managed by the utilization of psychotherapy, medication, or a combination of both. Various methods exist for managing anxiety, and it is advisable to collaborate with a healthcare professional in order to choose the most suitable course of treatment for your specific needs.

### Psychotherapy

Psychotherapy, also known as "talk therapy," is effective in assisting individuals with anxiety disorders. In order to achieve optimal results, psychotherapy must be focused on addressing your own fears and customized to cater to your unique requirements.

**Cognitive behavioral treatment**

Cognitive Behavioral Therapy (CBT) is a specific form of psychotherapy that can be beneficial for individuals suffering from anxiety disorders. It imparts many cognitive, behavioral, and emotional strategies to assist individuals in reducing their levels of anxiety and dread. Cognitive Behavioral Therapy (CBT) has undergone extensive research and is widely recognized as the most effective form of psychotherapy.

**Exposure therapy**

Exposure therapy is a cognitive-behavioral therapy technique employed for the treatment of anxiety disorders. Exposure treatment aims to address the underlying worries associated with an anxiety condition, enabling individuals to actively participate in activities they have been avoiding. Exposure therapy is occasionally employed in conjunction with relaxation exercises.

## Acceptance and commitment therapy (ACT)

Acceptance and commitment therapy (ACT) is an additional therapeutic alternative for certain anxiety disorders. The ACT method diverges from CBT in its attitude towards negative thoughts. The approach employs techniques such as mindfulness and goal setting to alleviate discomfort and anxiety.

ACT, being a more recent method of psychotherapy treatment in comparison to CBT, has limited data available regarding its effectiveness.

**Pharmaceutical treatment**

Medication cannot provide a cure for anxiety disorders, but it can assist in alleviating symptoms. Medical professionals, such as a psychiatrist or primary care practitioner, have the authority to prescribe medicine to treat anxiety. In many states, psychologists who have undergone specific training are also permitted to administer psychiatric drugs.

The predominant categories of drugs employed to address anxiety disorders are antidepressants, anxiolytics (such as benzodiazepines), and beta-blockers. Pharmaceuticals used to treat depression and related mental health conditions includes the following:

**Antidepressants:**

Antidepressants are used for the treatment of depression, and they can also be beneficial in managing anxiety disorders. They can enhance the brain's utilization of specific neurotransmitters that regulate mood or stress. It may be necessary to experiment with multiple antidepressant medications in order to discover the one that effectively alleviates your symptoms while also having tolerable side effects.

It is crucial to allow sufficient time for antidepressants to take effect before forming a judgment on their efficacy, as they may require several weeks to become effective. It is imperative to seek assistance from a healthcare professional before discontinuing the use of antidepressant medication. Your healthcare practitioner can assist you in gradually and securely reducing your dosage. Cessation of their use can result in the manifestation of withdrawal symptoms.

Children, teenagers, and individuals under the age of 25 may, in certain instances, encounter heightened tendencies towards suicide thoughts or actions when undergoing treatment with antidepressant medicines, particularly within the initial weeks after commencing the medication or when the dosage is altered. As a result, individuals of all age groups who are prescribed antidepressants should be constantly monitored, particularly in the initial weeks of medication.

**Anxiolytic drugs**

Anxiolytic medicines can effectively alleviate the symptoms associated with anxiety, panic attacks, or excessive dread and apprehension. Benzodiazepines are the most prevalent drugs used to treat anxiety.

While benzodiazepines are occasionally employed as initial therapies for generalized anxiety disorder, they possess both advantages and disadvantages.

Benzodiazepines exhibit efficacy in alleviating anxiety and demonstrate a faster onset of action compared to antidepressant drugs. Nevertheless, certain individuals develop a resistance to these drugs, necessitating progressively increasing doses to get the desired outcome. Certain individuals may develop a dependency on them. In order to mitigate these issues, healthcare professionals typically administer benzodiazepines for limited durations. Discontinuing benzodiazepines abruptly can result in the manifestation of withdrawal symptoms or the reoccurrence of anxiety. Consequently, it is advisable to gradually reduce the dosage of benzodiazepines.

## Beta-blockers

Beta-blockers, primarily prescribed for hypertension, can also alleviate the physiological manifestations of anxiety, including tachycardia, tremors, shaking, and facial flushing. These drugs can effectively manage physical symptoms when used for short durations. Additionally, they can be utilized on an as-needed basis to alleviate acute anxiety, including as a preventive measure for certain foreseeable manifestations of performance worries.

## Selecting the Appropriate Drug

Certain categories of medications may exhibit superior efficacy in treating particular forms of anxiety disorders. Consequently, individuals are advised to collaborate closely with a healthcare professional in order to ascertain the most suitable medication for their condition. Substances such as coffee, certain over-the-counter cold medicines, illicit narcotics, and herbal supplements have the potential to worsen the symptoms of anxiety disorders or have adverse effects when combined with prescribed medication. Individuals should engage in discussions with a healthcare professional in order to get knowledge about substances that are deemed safe and those that should be avoided. It is crucial to seek the guidance of a specialist when determining the appropriate drug, dosage, and treatment strategy. These decisions should be tailored to an individual's specific requirements and medical condition.

**Support groups**

Individuals suffering from anxiety disorders may find it advantageous to participate in a self-help or support group, where they can openly discuss their challenges and accomplishments with fellow members. Support groups are accessible through both physical and virtual means. Nevertheless, it is important to exercise caution when considering advice from a support group member, as it should not be regarded as a substitute for treatment suggestions provided by a healthcare professional.

## Methods for Effectively Managing Stress

Implementing stress management practices, such as engaging in physical exercise, practicing mindfulness, and engaging in meditation, can effectively alleviate symptoms of anxiety and amplify the benefits of psychotherapy. To gain further insight into the advantages of these procedures for your treatment, it is advisable to engage in a discussion with a healthcare professional.

## Therapeutic interventions for depression

Depression can be treated using three primary therapeutic approaches. The two most significant and extensively utilized treatments are psychotherapy and psychotropic medication, particularly antidepressants like bupropion. Psychotherapy seeks to modify the patient's maladaptive cognitive and behavioral reactions to stressful life situations, while also providing emotional assistance to the patient. In contrast, antidepressant medicines exert a direct influence on the brain's chemistry and are believed to alleviate depression by rectifying the chemical imbalance responsible for the condition.

## Post-Traumatic Stress Disorder (PTSD)

Post-traumatic stress disorder (PTSD) is a psychological issue that can arise following exposure to traumatic occurrences. The condition was initially identified in war veterans. In the past, it has been referred to by various names, including 'shell shock', but it is important to note that it is not exclusively diagnosed in soldiers. Post-traumatic stress disorder (PTSD), also known as post-traumatic stress syndrome, is an emotional condition that can occur after experiencing a traumatic event. This event is often one that involves the possibility of death or serious injury, leading to profound emotions of fear, helplessness, or horror. Post-traumatic stress disorder is characterized by the presence of symptoms such as distressing thoughts or memories of the trauma, and in severe cases, vivid recollections where the trauma is relived with intense emotions. Individuals with PTSD frequently describe a sense of emotional detachment, heightened anxiety and alertness, and a tendency to avoid triggers associated with their traumatic experiences, including certain situations, thoughts, and emotions. Experiencing certain reactions after a traumatic event is quite common, and they are not classified as signs of PTSD unless they persist for a minimum of one month or occur later on. Individuals with PTSD may also experience additional psychological challenges, such as depression, anxiety, and substance abuse. It is worth noting that the experience of traumatic stress is quite prevalent, with around ten percent of women and 5 percent of men encountering PTSD at some stage in their lives. The risk of developing PTSD can vary significantly depending on the type of trauma experienced. It is important to note that women are at a higher risk of developing PTSD after experiencing rape or other forms of sexual abuse. The disorder tends to manifest in individuals who have experienced significant trauma, lack adequate social support, and struggle to process their emotions and find a new perspective on their experiences.

After someone has developed PTSD, there are two highly effective treatments available: antidepressant medication and trauma reexposure. Trauma reexposure is a type of psychotherapy where the victim is encouraged to share their traumatic experience. By gradually revisiting the trauma in their memory, the goal is to help them change their emotional reactions and gain a new perspective on the experience.

# CHAPTER FIVE

## Low Self-esteem or Lacking Confidence

## in Oneself

Low self-esteem is characterized by a lack of confidence and a negative perception of oneself, feeling unworthy, inadequate, incompetent, unacceptable, or unlovable. Negative, self-critical thoughts can have a significant impact on your behavior and life choices, leading to a cycle of loneliness and frustration. Having low self-esteem can have a significant impact on a person's mental well-being, potentially resulting in feelings of stress, depression, and the development of eating disorders. It is crucial to act promptly when you become aware that you or a loved one is experiencing this debilitating issue.

## Strategies for Boosting Self-Confidence

Typically, low self-esteem is a result of learned behavior. It seems that the feelings of self-worth you're currently grappling with may have been influenced by external sources or may have originated from a tendency to dwell on your shortcomings. In order to address this learned behavior, it is important to embrace new beliefs and recognize that perfection is unattainable. Here are some helpful suggestions to boost your self-esteem and cultivate a more fulfilling life.

> ➢ Avoid the habit of constantly comparing yourself to others.

It's important to remember that you are not obligated to fulfill every societal expectation placed upon you. To overcome low self-esteem, it's important to prioritize living life on your own terms rather than constantly seeking validation from others. It's important to focus on your own accomplishments and not compare them to others. Instead, establish clear boundaries and set achievable goals to pursue your aspirations. Keep in mind that every individual possesses their own distinct qualities and contributions. Learning to stop comparing yourself to others can lead to a greater sense of happiness and contentment with oneself.

➢ Quiet the negative self-talk

Positive thinking is essential for building self-esteem. Negative thoughts can be a clear indicator of low self-esteem. When those thoughts come to mind, it's important to consider the alternative perspective. It may require some initial effort, but over time, you will naturally improve your ability to think positively. Thought patterns play a crucial role in determining our emotional well-being. If you lack confidence, it may be due to certain thoughts that make you question your worth. Take the time to identify the thoughts that are contributing to your feelings of low self-worth. It is essential to conduct a self-evaluation since only you have access to the inner workings of your mind.

➤ Enhance your current state

There are various factors that can contribute to a decrease in self-esteem. There are certain factors that you may not have control over, while there are others that you have the ability to change. Take body dysmorphia, for instance. It can really take a toll on your self-esteem. If you're looking to make positive changes to your health, one option is to incorporate a regular exercise routine like mindful walking and adopt mindful eating habits. By incorporating regular exercise and a balanced diet into your lifestyle, you will experience a multitude of beneficial transformations in both your physical well-being and appearance. For some individuals, this can serve as an excellent initial step towards enhancing their self-esteem. If you find that constant fatigue is affecting your self-esteem, consider making a simple change to your routine.

Try switching off your computer and television a few hours earlier each night, allowing yourself the opportunity to get a solid 8 hours of restful sleep. This small adjustment can make a big difference in how you feel. Discover a night time routine that effortlessly helps you relax and unwind before bed. Getting enough sleep is essential for maintaining a healthy mind and body.

You'll experience a refreshing start to your day, feeling energized and ready to tackle whatever comes your way.

> ➤ Have confidence in your decisions

It's important to prioritize your health and avoid doubting your decisions. This is not a healthy choice to make for yourself. If you find yourself in the company of toxic individuals and it negatively affects your well-being, it's important to address the situation rather than enduring the mistreatment, especially if it indicates underlying self-esteem issues. Instead, it would be best to remove those individuals from your life. Improving confidence becomes more attainable when a resolute decision is made. The resolution of these concerns ultimately hinges on your ability to truly hear and trust your own inner voice.

> ➤ Experience something different

Many individuals who struggle with low self-esteem often experience a sense of inadequacy or a belief that they are not meeting expectations. They believe they are unable to achieve certain things. Unfortunately, this often becomes a reality. To overcome low self-respect, it's important to recognize your untapped potential. As you embark on exciting new experiences and acquire new abilities, your confidence will continue to grow. As you gain experience, you'll discover that there are endless possibilities when you have faith in your abilities.

> ➢ Consult with a mental health professional

It is advisable for individuals facing self-esteem challenges to seek guidance from a mental health expert. Boosting a person's self-esteem can be quite challenging, especially when it stems from past experiences of childhood trauma. Parents who provide an imbalanced amount of praise can sometimes contribute to self-esteem issues in their children. It is important to seek the help of a professional when dealing with mental health issues like this. Examining how your parents evaluated you in relation to your siblings or other children can sometimes lead to challenges with self-confidence.

# Addressing Low Self-Esteem Issues

When overcoming low self-esteem, it's important not to let negative emotions control you. Take a stand and conquer any obstacles by following your own path. Before you realize it, your confidence will soar, propelling you towards the realization of your dreams.

> ➢ Assist individuals

The answer to having a healthy self-esteem is to increase it via acts of kindness and good deeds. If you find it difficult to recognize your excellent attributes, simply focus on enhancing and showcasing them. By providing assistance, offering encouragement during victories, and maintaining a general attitude of support, you will receive a considerable amount of favorable feedback. By improving the lives of another individual, you will receive numerous benefits as a result. Gradually, although steadily, your self-esteem will enhance. You will have increased self-compassion as a result of recognizing the level of exertion you are investing. Strive to perform acts of kindness on a daily basis, and don't hesitate to seek out chances online where you may spread kindness. In the end, you'll notice your mind improve because you're not in your head anymore, you're too busy living in the real environment that you're constructing to be a better experience for yourself.

➤ Identify defensive mechanisms

A defense mechanism refers to an automatic and unconscious response to a particular event. Various defense mechanisms exist, including projection, denial, repression, and others. When experiencing guilt, individuals often employ defense mechanisms as a means of safeguarding themselves against internalizing negative actions, ideas, or life experiences. Individuals with diminished self-esteem often employ protection mechanisms unconsciously. It is conceivable that an accumulation of numerous adverse occurrences has impacted your self-esteem and led you to shield yourself from further unfavorable encounters. Nevertheless, we all employ defense systems at some stage. Ensure that you acknowledge and identify the behavior when you observe yourself engaging in it, in order to prevent difficulties from arising in the future.

> ➢ Attempt to achieve a state of calmness and relaxation.

A persistent sensation of tension is one of the factors that contribute to low self-esteem. It is crucial to understand the art of relaxation. During periods of stress, your mind becomes dominated by negative thoughts, causing you to direct your attention on your deficiencies rather than your strengths. This will exacerbate your stress levels and further contribute to diminished self-esteem. Allocate a portion of your schedule to engage in an activity that brings you a sense of calm and tranquility. Engage in self-care activities. Engage in activities such as bathing, playing video games, practicing guided meditation, singing, or engaging in indoor dance. Implementing this will alleviate your tension and enhance your self-esteem.

➢ Embrace the present moment

To combat low self-esteem, one can adopt the practice of living in the present moment and refraining from allowing previous traumas or future anxieties to influence one's behavior. To accomplish this, actively involve your five senses. Take a moment to listen attentively to the harmonious sounds of birds, perceive the gentle touch of the air on your skin, inhale the invigorating scent of the atmosphere, and appreciate the captivating hue of the sky. Engaging in these activities will focus your awareness on the present moment and cultivate a mindset conducive to making sound daily choices.

➢ Show compassion towards yourself

What is the reason for exhibiting kindness towards others while being self-critical? One effective strategy for healing low self-esteem is to adopt a compassionate, tender, and forgiving attitude towards oneself, similar to how one would treat a close friend. Compassion Meditation is a method of sitting and dedicating time to cultivate self-love and kindness.

Occasionally, we may exhibit generosity towards our friends and family, yet fail to apply that same care towards ourselves. Embrace your true self, cultivate self-love, and witness a significant boost in your self-esteem.

> ➢ Enumerate your positive attributes

Pessimistic thoughts can hinder your ability to recognize the positive qualities you possess. One might enhance their self-esteem by documenting all their positive attributes. You have the option to seek assistance from a friend or even your relatives. Solicit positive comments from individuals to enhance your self-awareness on the qualities that others appreciate in you.

Consider compiling a catalog of commendable behaviors that you possess as well. Utilize this exercise as a means to cultivate and enhance your ability to show kindness, understanding, and acceptance towards yourself.

> Avoid excessive rumination on errors.

Internal thoughts have the potential to undermine one's self-esteem. You have personal obligations to fulfill. Instead of allowing yourself to engage in repetitive and self-destructive ideas, make an effort to intercept negative thoughts at their origin. Being cognizant of the mental processes occurring in your brain is crucial in achieving this. Whenever a pessimistic notion arises in your mind, utter the word "halt." Surprisingly, it significantly aids in being mentally and emotionally engaged in the current moment rather than dwelling on past events or worrying about future uncertainties. It restores your sense of agency. Additionally, individuals with low self-esteem might elevate their approach by substituting negative thinking with positive beliefs. Keep in mind that negative ideas are merely beliefs, devoid of reality.

 Errors will persist throughout your lifetime; the key is to extract valuable lessons from them. There is no necessity to criticize or feel inadequate, each time you make a mistake. Do not allow fear to interfere with your learning experience.

➢ Immerse yourself in the company of those who exude positivity.

Our self-esteem is greatly influenced by the perceptions and information we receive about ourselves. Occasionally, those things can have a lasting impact. Whether you realize it or not, the individuals with whom you have surrounded yourself or engaged in interactions in the past have had a significant role in shaping the person you have become now.

If your goal is to cultivate a positive self-image, why would you choose to associate with others who harbor self-loathing? Why form a friendship with an individual who harbors self-deprecation or lacks aspirations, ambitions, or a sense of direction in life?

> ➤ Acquire more knowledge

If your self-perception is accurate and you are apprehensive about having inadequate self-esteem due to feelings of inadequacy, it is imperative to cease detrimental behaviors and cultivate novel abilities. The treatment for self-esteem will ultimately involve implementing constructive modifications. Most advise will assert that you possess inherent perfection. And that is accurate to a certain degree. However, wouldn't life be enhanced by continuously striving to enhance oneself? There is no inherent issue with striving for improvement. If you are experiencing verbal confrontations with individuals, it would be beneficial for you to engage in reading literature on communication. If you are perceived as unpleasant by others, you can attempt to engage in more benevolent actions towards others. If individuals mock your attire, you might peruse information about fashion to enhance your clothing choices.

> Refrain from engaging in self-deprecating behavior.

While striving to conquer your diminished self-worth, bear in mind that we are all fallible beings. Every individual, at some juncture in their existence, will inevitably commit an error. Indeed, certain individuals earn far more incomes than others. One effective strategy for conquering low self-esteem is to cultivate the ability to refrain from self-criticism when encountering errors or failures. On the contrary, get knowledge from that error. Commit this information to your mind and utilize it as a means of avoiding the repetition of the same error in the future. It is important to remember that we acquire knowledge through the process of experimentation and making mistakes.

Resolving low self-esteem requires a considerable amount of effort and patience. Undoubtedly, there may be occasions when you experience a sense of stagnation or perceive your efforts as unproductive. There will also be occasions when you will feel discouraged and desire to connect with those individuals who lack a sense of direction in life. Do not allow these instances to impede your progress on your path. Rise and persist through your obstacles, and ultimately, you will attain your objectives and have a contented, prosperous existence.

# CHAPTER SIX

## Diet, Exercise, Physical Activities and Mental Well-being

The interplay between diet, exercise, and sleep is intricate and multifarious. Gaining knowledge about the interplay between these activities is a crucial aspect of comprehending the research findings that indicate an enhancement in well-being with an increase in the number of improved lifestyle behaviors.

Frequently, those who engage in regular physical activity do so primarily due to the positive impact it has on their well-being. Physical activity has the potential to enhance your emotional state, focus, and vigilance. It can also contribute to fostering an optimistic perspective on life. The relationship between physical activity and mental health is intricate. Inactivity can serve as both a catalyst and a result of mental illness, as an illustrative instance. Exercise offers numerous ways to enhance your mental well-being, including:

> Exercise induces alterations in the neurochemical composition of the brain, including serotonin, stress hormones, and endorphins.

> Engaging in regular physical activity can enhance your quality of sleep. Furthermore, adequate sleep facilitates the regulation of your emotional state.

> Engaging in physical activity can enhance your perception of agency, capacity to manage stress, and self-worth. Frequent exercisers frequently express the positive emotions they

experience upon accomplishing a goal.

➤ Engaging in physical activity might divert your attention from pessimistic thoughts and offer chances to explore novel encounters.

➤ Exercising with others provides a chance to engage in social interactions and receive social assistance.

➤ Physical activity enhances your levels of energy.

➤ Engaging in physical activity can serve as a means to release and channel your tensions.

➤ Physical activity has the ability to decrease skeletal muscular tension, leading to a heightened sense of relaxation.

The physiological advantages of physical activity are as crucial for individuals with mental illness. It enhances your cardiovascular well-being and general physical fitness. This is significant because individuals with mental health disorders are more susceptible to experiencing persistent physical ailments, including heart disease, diabetes, arthritis, and asthma.

# Impact of Nutritional Regimen on Mental Health

The impact of diet and nutrition on an individual's health is comprehensive and far-reaching. Consuming a nutritious and well-rounded diet has been proven to decrease the likelihood of several health ailments, such as cardiovascular disease, cerebrovascular accident, diabetes, and obesity. Research indicates that specific dietary choices can influence mental well-being, perhaps decreasing the likelihood of experiencing despair and anxiety.

Optimal consumption of water, carbs, and protein at appropriate intervals can enhance athletic performance and reduce weariness. Indulging in unhealthy food options, such as consuming a meal immediately prior to engaging in a vigorous cardiovascular exercise, might result in heightened feelings of nausea and render physical activity more arduous.

For optimal growth and development of children, it is crucial to have a diet that includes whole grains, vegetables, fruits, dairy products, and plant proteins. Nevertheless, the growing accessibility of detrimental, processed foods and the inactive behaviors stemming from prolonged use of electronic devices pose significant obstacles to attaining these healthful lifestyle practices.

In children of all ages, the consumption of sweets, snacks, and sugar-sweetened drinks is linked to sedentary behavior and poor levels of physical activity. This, in turn, raises the likelihood of developing obesity and cardiovascular disease.

The independence and autonomy experienced throughout young adulthood frequently worsen bad eating patterns and the absence of physical activity. This is due to the challenges faced by young people in allocating time to prioritize a healthy diet and exercise, given the mounting academic and social obligations and hectic schedules. These detrimental lifestyle habits heighten the likelihood of developing obesity and cardiovascular disease in the future.

## Rest

Sleep provides the body and brain with an opportunity to rejuvenate and recuperate, impacting almost every tissue in the body. The majority of adults require a minimum of seven hours of sleep, but, about one-third of Americans are obtaining less than this recommended amount. Insufficient sleep heightens the likelihood of developing health ailments such as diabetes, cardiovascular disease, and stroke. Extended sleep deprivation can also impact focus and other cognitive abilities. Inadequate sleep often leads individuals to engage in excessive eating and make unfavorable dietary choices. Sleep deprivation impacts the body's secretion of ghrelin and leptin, which are two neurotransmitters that regulate the brain's appetite for calories. Individuals experiencing sleep deprivation exhibit a greater inclination towards consuming high-calorie items. Chronic sleep deprivation has been associated with a greater waist circumference and an elevated risk of obesity. Sleep provides a crucial period for muscle tissue to recuperate and regenerate after intense physical activity. Adequate sleep is crucial for maintaining the necessary energy levels to engage in physical activity. Inadequate sleep might result in decreased physical activity throughout the day and diminished muscular strength during exercise sessions. Sleep deprivation can also compromise the safety of physical activity, as those who are sleep deprived have been found to experience a higher incidence of sports-related injuries.

Although nutrition and exercise are widely recognized as crucial factors for enhancing one's health, the significance of sleep is sometimes disregarded. Implementing sleep hygiene practices, which encompass behaviors that enhance the quality of sleep, can serve as an initial step towards enhancing your sleep.

**Do not eat too late:** Be sure to give your body time to digest after eating substantial meals. Consider shifting your meal time to an earlier hour in the evening.

Avoid the consumption of caffeine: Exercise caution when consuming stimulants such as coffee, energy drinks, and soda. If you choose to drink these, endeavor to restrict their consumption to the morning hours.

**Engage in physical activity:** Establish a consistent exercise routine to enhance the quality of your sleep. Although any physical activity during daylight hours is advantageous, strive to engage in consistent, moderate exercise several times each week. Avoid exercising in close proximity to bedtime, allowing your body a few hours to relax and unwind before sleep.

Obtain natural light: Engage in physical activity outside, as being exposed to natural light during the day can assist in maintaining your body's alignment with its inherent sleep patterns.

**END**

www.ingramcontent.com/pod-product-compliance
Lightning Source LLC
Chambersburg PA
CBHW060944260726
48661CB00005B/1749